D1881474

So The Time Passed Away

So The Time Passed Away

Meanderings of a vagrant soul so long ago

Professor C B S R Sharma

GenNext Publication

© **Author**

All rights reserved. No part of this work may be reproduced, stored, adapted, or transmitted in any form or by any means, electronic, mechanical, photocopying, micro-filming, recording or otherwise, or translated in any language, without the prior written permission of the copyright owner and the publisher. The book is sold subject to the condition that it shall not, by way of trade or otherwise, be lent, resold, hired out, or otherwise circulated without the prior publisher's written consent in any form of binding or cover other than that in which it is published.

The views and opinions expressed in this book are author(s) own and the facts reported by them have been verified to the extent possible, and the publishers are not in any way liable for the same.

ISBN: 978-93-5324-644-0 (HB)

"An Imprint of Kalpaz Publications"

First Published, 2021

Published by

GenNext Publication
5, Ansari Road
Daryaganj, New Delhi-110002
Phone: 9811692060
E-mail: gennextpublication@hotmail.com

Printed at: Gyan Press, Delhi.

The angel
that presided over my birth
Said

**"Little Creature,
formed of joy and mirth,
Go, work and love
Without the help
of anything on earth"**

– *Blake*

DEDICATION

CYRIL ANTONY
A Rare Good Soul
in Pondicherry

Tower of BITS Pilani and
Prof. Babu Narhar Muley,
The Gurus of the Author

Acknowledgments

Lothar Wendel, Damstadt, Germany
Pranab Ray, Calcutta
Padmanabha Rao, Hyderabad

And

Javed Sultan of Dharbhanga
Now at Delhi with Gyan
For his Enthusiastic Feelings
And Remembering
Sahir Ludhianvi and Sadat Manto

This book is a Complimentary
by the Publishers

Preface

THEN

My father died. Worried about a mother and four siblings.
My professor died. I Myself became an Orphan

Feelings of loneliness engulf and spread in all directions.
Cannot express either orally or in writing.

Yet reams and reams come in a few sentences
and phrases. These were identified as poetry by
Pranab Ray and supported by Lothar Wendel and
Padmanabha Rao.

This is the birth of my Jottings.

NOW

Globalisation – designing injustices and sorrows to
be seen by the blind and heard by the deaf.
This fitted in a society where health, education and
justice were always ignored.

Now everyone tries to find a victim to profit from !
Those pieces of pain and hope become relevant in
double measure, for, there appears no hope!

Just as Pranab then, Cyril now continuously egged
on me to make public these private beats

When fate appears a fixed star and joy a vane that
veers, I chose the title "*So the time passed away*"
as a homage to Bertholt Brecht.

Birla Institute of Technology and Science [1965 – 70]

Contents

1. Ecology

Each organism gives what it can
And takes what it needs
Patience is extreme,
When lost anger irreversible
Cause here effect there
Cause now effect later,
Everything is connected,
It is powerful, it is fragile,
Some one prepares food,
Some one consumes,
Someone else nourishes
It is useful, it is harmful
Thus commons are strengthened
for common good

2. Helm of the Chariot

The birds are pricking the clouds
My fingers slightly waved her lovelocks
There was a drizzle, there was a trickle
My enchantress laughed and tickled my core
The cuckoo had a dip in the stream of love
The crows of the dirt poked their beaks in vain
The balls of my eyes were rolling in waters
While the glows of passion swam to the shores of Cupid
I thought I landed in an ambush, but
It was only the preface for a rosy advent

At last the petals of crimson spread a welcome path
And the mountains started a retreat
Today I see the peaks aglow
The marble mounds are hard to mould
I feared their mount
And the confidence was in tremor
But I felt their caress for me
Heavens! I have nothing to bother under the sky
But to live a life of peace
For the Goddess of sun at the helm of the chariot.

3. Charm of the Seasons

Oh! meadow of flower-filled tresses
Don't enchant me with sapling smiles
And lure me with lullabies of spring
Oh! sky of pregnant clouds
Don't pour down the streams of flowers
And the charms of Pendanus petals

Hibiscus vied in your trail
And in the gardens of your songs
Amorous romances paraded in full spate
The beauties of chrysanthemums in your body
And in your manes
The pervasions of dark sky

You laughed at me
There was a train of moonlight
You wept for me, and
There was a rain in torrents
You made me cry
And then laughed aloud
For you kept within your hold
The charms of all the seasons

4. Agony of the Deserted

The rich mountains once they were
Are the one to shed for me
Life disheveled, reduced to mere mounds
In the ghastly glare of summer scorch
They are pretty, petty dunes of tomorrow
What if thousand petals flower
What if thousand more flourish
When what is wanting is fragrance

The brooking stream, once it was
Is the one to shed for me
The flow of life receding, and virginity shrunken
In the arid blows of sandy desert
They are the dauntless depressions of tomorrow
What if hundred waters fall
What if hundred more flame
When what is wanting is a buoyant flow

Where to look for? What to seek?
Where are my saviours? Where are my benefactors?
Can a beam of light reach me?
Can I nurture the luxury of hope?
And feel the light
When the dawn is still dark
I am the people of today and yesterday
Tombed forever for the fear of awakening

5. The Santal Woman

A santal woman looks at herself.
Half naked, bare footed and bones mocking
The shriveled hair bundled into a bun of patience
And over her hips a basket wealth of compassion

The santal woman gazes behind.
A police dances at the ashes of her hut
A marauder plays music for the dying victim
And a jackal watches wistful with its moist tongue

The santal woman searches herself.
The ragged garments flew to wipe the tears
The naked feet walked fast to help the lame
The bared bones marched to relieve the hunger

The santal woman raises from the slumber.
Repels adaptation and rejects the detachment.
A woman aroused is stranger than the devil.
And a weak aroused is mightier than the evil.

The santal woman rediscovers herself
The deep forest drew her toward
The basket carries the breath of men
The grenades within left a smile, a trail of venture

6. I Shall

I shall suggest to the stars
To spring up as the jasmines
In the dark plait of my girl

I shall request the twines of lightning
To glow as floods of smiles
On the lips of my love

I shall beg the clouds
To dance as a flock of ringlets
On the forehead of my beloved

I shall plead before the sky
To spread as a silken wear
On the curven profile of my darling

7. The Destined Shore

The winds of Vales swept
The hearts into violent throbs
Like the river in spate
Flooded the carnal desire over me
The green of youth served
A pawn to the effervescent beauty
Adorning the bunch of jasmines
Laughed the braid of darkness
As the masts of hope rose in chorus
The boat sailed to the destined shores

8. I Long for Tussles

It is the day I long
A day without a drizzle
From my beloved's drenching lips
When the smiles fall out
What do I wish than a scorching sun

It is the night I hope
The night without a moonlight
From my darling's countenance
When the rays resplendent beam out
What do I love than a fathomless darkness

It is the evening I wait
The one without a breeze
From the heartbeats of my sweetheart
When my life's purpose is carved out
I but order the air to a standstill

It is the morrow I invite
The morn marching with chaos
From the faith of my better half
When strength nestles in my heart
I ever long for tussles

9. The Woman

Woman
The riplet of the buzzing wind
Smiling like a wing of crescent
Sings the flying bird
Like the atoning string of life

Woman
The floret of the morn
Dancing like a buoyant brook
Hangs to the twig of prop
Like a warming ken of promise

Woman
The ray of flickering beam
Flaming like a cascade flake
Alights the cursing black
Like a candle of burning hope

Woman
The pervading fragrance
Singing like a noisy breezelet
Ushers a forceful zeal
Like a sweeping gale of clarion

10. Dawn or Darkness

I know you well
And knowing you, I feel an ecstatic pain
Pain, because of being the fountain of troubles
No longer can I deceive myself
When blood and sweat are damned and demolished
Hence is this honourable course
When dishonour came to me unjustified
When a sting of infamy is tagged to you

I cannot offer you anything
But a remnant gesture of heart
I cannot protect you
With the strength of position or wealth
I can only smear you with my weaknesses
For I love you
And loving you
I realise its logical end

The last leg of journey marches fast
Obvious, the sun is kissing my hours
I am eager
Whether it is of dawn or darkness

11. We are Born Dying

Rainbow crept into the rain of dreams
The horizon serene
And clouded with no mist
Is it the end of suffering
And the dawn of a new era?
Or a warning to the civilisation
A call for suffering unto the end?

Battered bat-like
In the summer blaze
Littled into a straw
In the torrents of rain
Shrunken to nothing
In the wintry cold
And hardened with hunger

Ululated with throngs of pain
Into the desert of humanity
A protest that is also a prophecy
To be born is a crime
And to die another
But committed is only one
For we are born dying

12. The Paradox

Have you seen the invisible tears
Bubbling in the smiles of million mouths
The mouths of hope

Have you seen the alluding wealth
Lurking in the rags of the street beggar
The street of progress

Have you seen the smouldering fire
Buried in the blinded eyes of ire
The eyes of vision

Have you seen the transparent poverty
In the pervasions of the miasmic affluence
The affluence of plunder

The thirst abounds
When the rivers are in floods
And there shall be no famines
When the lands are strolled by vermin
Life is a contradiction
And living, a paradox

13. The Trumpet

Even I did
In the sacrificial pyre of the world
Subscribe a candle of glow.

Even I did
In the celestial rain of cosmos
Diffuse a tear of contrition.

Even I did
Into the clarion of the horizons
Plunge my tongue in madness.

Then I will
In the lotus of civilisation
Revel as its pivotal petal.

Then I will
In the sitar of life
Absorb myself as its string.

Then I will
On the foundations of the new dawn
Throw the beacon onto the firmament.

14. When and How

I saw you
Seeing you
My sight refuses anything else
Departing from me
Shall I be left blind, or
Rays I shall see How soon?

Sleep came to me through rails
On your lap over the red silk
My heart knows no rest ever since
And my mind no respite
Sleep pitiless unless through your thighs.
How long shall I be on the wait for a wink?

Departing from the abode of our union
You sapped my strength and stamina
I am a straw, straw in a stream
Sleepless and sightless
Sans strength, sans prop.
When will you bring my life ?

15. Letters

Letters, letters of infinite variety
Musing and amusing
Frightening and flattering
Boasting and bowing
Those are fortunate
For whom are letters
To and fro books
Like flood flow their friendship.

Letters, letters of umpteen types
Some weeding out worry
Many feeding in happy
Like parrots they speak
The bonds of friendship
Like compass they point
The marks of kinship
Between friends of common goal.

Letters, letters of varied forms
Strolls in imagination
Seeds of impatient longings
Factors in probing minds
Places of meeting hearts
These lifeless creatures
Better the humans
In a myriad ways.

16. Ah! Ah! Ah!

Emitting fires of resplendence
When I flew to the skies
With all swollen eyes
With all surprise
These people, these people ....
Hailed me with full throats.

Defeated, crest fallen and vomiting blood
When I fell to the ground
With all revenge, qualmless
With all hatred, merciless
The same people, the same people ......
Devoured me with full vigour.

And this is Humanity!

17. Wakeful Eyes

In the cool interior of the ocean depths
Devouring fires of revenge lie hidden
In the blue sheath of the skies
The raising suns have taken refuge.

For the birth of the earth
Heavens panged in despair.
The advent of man is a Saga
Of a myriad painful convulsions.

Throats are slain
In the victory, but of a mortal king
In the vortex of religion
Few are spared from perdition.

In the kissing waves of the beach
The winds of change gallop ashore
In the gale of lightnings
The slumber will have its sunset.

In the infant's wakeful eyes
Lie the promise of future.
In the heart of a broken poet
Lie loads of unwritten wisdom.

18. My Words

My words
Are damsels of beauty
Playing in the streams of moonlight.

My words
Are mountains of kindness
Drenching in the torrents of tears.

My words
Are elephants of victory
Pervading the spirit of masses.

My words
Are whirls of hurricane
Throwing the people into action.

19. The Inevitable East

Morning silence
Serenades the murky graveyard
The bazaar ballyhoo
Lulls the examination room

The bloodier toys without a tool
And the male languishes in suspicion
The leader lolls on a wayward road
And the following swell with spite
The old and the young
Blinded and visionless

Dead mounds abound the provision store
And spineless profiles silhouette the street

The roses on the Capparis
Vies with the spiny Chrysanthemum
The grains dupe their gatherer
And the product outwits its hammerer
The dog licks the master
While the clock ticks lazily

There is clarity in the sundown
And a black night in the evening bells
Meanwhile the phosphorescence from the outskirts
Marches towards the inevitable east

20. Cascade and the Caravan

The cascade of typhoons
Wait on the stillness of air
I am a prophet of doom
My intuition works on the negative front

If I had become stale
If my shadow became an affront
You can burn my memory with ease
Lest incense lacks in my ashes

For ash is the end of sense
When confidence keeps distance from promise
The caravan of graveyards
Needs deserts to course on

21. The Price and the Value

I know
The price I have to pay
For everything I do
For everyone I come in contact
But…

I have yet to realise
The value
of anything I am expected to do
Of anybody who comes around me

When I fell
And eagles clamour for my rotten flesh
And dogs quarrel over my hollow bones
When told of this
She said:

What can I do when he is like that.
I am lovelorn
Being so
Must I be forlorn

22. The Glow of Twenty One

On the endless stream of life
I strolled a day and thought:
This fathomless stream is bankless too
And none would dare to help my straw across
And went ahead alone and stoic, while
The casuarinas blew their serenades
The cataracts of dew twitched their eyes
The waves made an issue with the pilgrim

I grew angry and restive alternately
And in a granted moment
Disturbed the waters of calm
There was a flutter among the barnacles
The Chemmeen rose out of Chakara
The fisherman came running with nets of catch
Gaping inquisitive at my unconcern
The shades of whales, I beheld with awe

But I found a gaze among the molluscans
The seashell came running and stood in front
And bowed with sepulchral smiles
The pearls inside busy with their birth pangs
The glows of the twenty-one
Ranged to illumine a desolate dungeon

23. Who are you?

Who are you?
Oh who are you?

You came to me with the sails of breeze
When my breath was ebbing in the air
You brought me the masts of direction
When my life was tossing in the Spasm of despair

Who are you?
Oh who are you?

The wandering crescent
Behind the veil of clouds
The resplendent starlet
On the descending firmament
The raising gait of the wave
In the coying mists of ripples
The flamboyance of the dancing bubble
In the infinity of the ocean
Compass of the stranded traveler
Candle in the fortress of darkness
Cataract of the dew
And the serenade of the palm

Who are you?
Oh who are you?
The symphony of the calls woke me up
The message landed in my yard
They flew from me in the morn
And nestled in yours at the dusk

Oh heart of my heart
And mind of my mind
You are my bloom, and
You are my spring

24. To the other Bank

The lamp that shone in my life
The flicker that kindled hope against hope
Waned and vanished in despair
The grotesque fears in the candle - less life

Clarion that moved into action
Raised its voice as a maestro
And lost its stretch into oblivion
The ill tuned voices from the stranded string

The pervasions of the Bunyan shade
Impelled me from the serpent vile
The stray wind stormed the trunk
At the ken are the colourful shades of life and death

Across the river I am
Coursing on a dauntless boat
Haunted by darkness, death and distress
Struggling their way onto me

My journey over the ferry, arduous and exacting
The dance macabre of shadows and cymbals
Foundered and found vent into darkness
At the glitter and glare of the splashing revolt

Misted out at the streaming sight
Of the raising beacon, littled into
A mystic vapour while I anchor my voyage
On the sum of light, love and life

Surprised at the new dawn
Eagerness and relief inquired where
Did I go last night. Thundered on the sky............

...To the other bank.

25. Time does not Brood

I can behold the end of distance
But not withhold the overtaking peak
For, the destination is thick with mist

Time has stopped ticking
Today my life is tired
The wound has bucked up again
Although it was a closed chapter
Once more the spring awoke
As the hill shines atop

The mind has ceased to think
The body is unable to move a foot
As I come to know of the truth
I turned dreadful to myself
The agony of parting is still licking
As the peaks are changing their hues

My confidence is shaken
My efforts are stilling me
The hopes of the world
Today, are living a vain life
Somewhere my foot landed on a thorn
And I am not aware of it

As the peaks at a distance
Are melting into the oblivion
Bewildered I gaze at the drying river
For I could do but little
To stop the galloping mare
Time does not brood but awaits the impending

26. The Ordain of the Times

I do not know
What your lips murmured
I do not know
What my drums received
But we know
Our thoughts mingled

The day has no sunshine
The night is not moonlit
No winds of cold embrace me
As the rainbow is still under the veil
The heat in me is tiding in tempest
For, your chariot of charms
Travel through the trickling
And my radiations shall pierce
Through the chills of all walls

When the silvery droplets
Fall on the hair traveling all the way
And drizzle over the snowy bosoms
By the splashes of the wavy ringlets
The passage of my nimble fingers
With the method of madness
Over the brooks of black tresses
Coursing the stratum of ivory
Unmask the vapour into the horizon in front
The tempest of love has its harvest

The crescent of your forehead
Lits the reluctant starlets of the teeth
While the clouds of the fingers
Make a vain attempt to hide
The charm of the seasons
The impending is inevitable
For the gods of passion
Ravaged the world of youth
And today
Is the fair of romance

On the path of passion
At last I am lost
So too you, I hope
For we have not remained what we were
Yet, we have a wait at the inns of time
For, it stored for us the sweetmeats of destiny

27. The Sprawling Stream

The dying sun vomits breathless
The horizon sprang serene and listless
As the east wind sank into the west
Leaving behind a thick gleam of hues
And I have the privilege to witness
The fanfare of the philistine pageant

The spawning desert in front
Reminds me the state of hunger
The scattered trees of the sands
Show me the sight of wrangling men
The frightening clouds above
Bespeak the pervasive tentacles
At the straws of gaping life

Once was a forest of innocent depth
The shady clouds descended with dizzy fumes
And now is a dead mound of sands
Yet the remnants remain in idyllic squatting
Ignorant of the story of their lineage
They laugh at the sands below
Having little monition of their own fate

The powdered muds yawned an anguish
For they have no voice to raise
In the stream of time they had a strawless swim
The alluring colours of the gallows
Jaundiced them to blindness
Their dumb wailing struggles to vomit
The kind of fate stored for the remainder of their kind.

The veil of darkness slowly descends
The scaffold sky hovers with dark and saffron
The moon and the stars fluttered from the drama
Sands jump and whin against the cursed dumbness
A solitary creeper smells and sighs
Will the glow of the lone traveler
Survive the treacherous winds and demonic pervasions

Oh! miasmic throng of servility!
Behold the clock on the tower at a distance
It denotes not the paralysis of time
But progress of the pilgrim
Don't you see the red lamp ahead?
It burns not you into quicksands
But lands you on the decks of prosperity
Oh! solitary but mighty life!
Before the bayonets of darkness pierce through
And tombed under the spoils of exploitation
Before the tumultuous gale yawns
And defeating thunders bugle to plunder
Unite under the banner of eternal flame
And glow with the rays of peace and prosperity.

28. The Ticks of Progress

Sunken motionless
In the fathomless darkness
The street lamp renders its duty
The dome of prop and refuge
Is spread from the dutiful servant
The shades of the angels
Mingled in the ghosts of mid-day sun.

Lying tailless with a broken leg
The orphaned mongrel of the street
Is dying for a look of pity
Palms wagging in wailing
To serve the tears of sympathy
The humidity of the eyes
Harbouring harsh rays of fire.

Wallowed into the lap of the mother earth
By the carnal fatigue of the lustful riffraff
The damsel in the nature's attire
Voiceless, extends the begging hand
For a patch of quilt under the packet of bones
In the lands of plenty, in the dearthless society
Missing is a twitch of mercy.

Under the breathless servility
The back-bent son of the soil
The bone-left man of the factory
The twin fathers of the world's wealth
Have too many a scared saviour
To aid a tongue for their last cry
The caravan of corpses defies the blinding storms

The carcass of mercy
Washed off in the cascade of thunderbolts
The music of death cries
Spawned in the yawn of hurricane
The tailless canine stands in tears
At the screaming shades of skeletons
Under the flicker of the wayside lamp.

In this world of boundless sounds
Under the reign of graveyard philosophy
There is dearth for a clarion
The small and the big of the clock
Round and around in vying flock
The strokes of the time
Are the only compass of progress.

29. Wastelands and Fertile Fields

I wished to be the hangman
Or the martyr in the noose
But ever my life had been
The curse of the martyr.
And I lived in the hangman's rope
And now let the casket empty itself

Thirst drives me towards the cup of life
Hunger reels me to the food in front
I want to live I want to live
Although the cup is empty and the dish is stale.

Morning star ——
Glowing with dying lustre
Gives dawn to the dusky lives
And is done with at the time of sunkiss.

Pathless time ——
The lone traveler on an eternal journey
On whom are thrown
Pebbles and flowers with fury and gusto.

Buoyant river —
Gives the essence of life
Although the wiser walk over it
At the times of its misfortune.
Enigmatic sky —
The canopy, where only
The pregnant clouds are dark
And the birds of charm fly in peace.

No star, no time, no river, no sky.
Can I be at least a flower of grass?
Living at the mercy of feminine winds
For, I give the grain to all who can grab.

Or have I to live as the light
Amplifying the good so less in the cup
Or shall I die as the darkness
Hiding all the bad so much in the plate ?

30. Triumph of Humanism

A Homage to Count Stauffenberg

The land of the German is the land of man
The urge of the man is the peace in unity
But the paths of heaven pass through dungeons of hell
And the story of Deutschland is the story of the worlk

The decade of sway and storm
Lulled the masses and lured the mound
The mansions of humanity, the toil of civilisations
Bulldozed by the insolence of the madding crowd

Bismarck's agony rose in his grave
To wipe the tears of his forlorn goals
The land of the Germans turns a mother of gallows
Where were no walls, yield no place without walls

The unity of man, the premise of universe
Toned in full throat by the clarion of Goethe
The orient and the occident, the old and the new
Fell to the blinding storms of the meridian blaze

No cheers to Max Mueller, no waves to Keyserling
They are spared for the heroes of Auschwitz
And to the bush above the drunken lips
The melodies of Bach, the beats of heart
Are dried in the din of warlord's drums
Reverence for life is the chosen epitaph for Schweitzer

The science is the anchor of prosperity
The Nazi science is the scaffold for the posterity
The pride of Germany, Oh! Einstein
Your sighs in the barn went unheeded

The atom of the scientist, string of the maestro
The word of the scholar and the whiteness of the horse
When put to abuse by the hordes of Hitler
The glory of the gene rises against the prophets of doom
To remind the world the existence of the other kind

There was a man with the laurels for victory
But itching for the blood of the master, the murderer
The looks reaching far the frontiers of Europe
The nose probing into the depth of depths

The lips as tight as the vessels airtight
And as bright as the hours of sunkiss
The left out eye and the spared fingers ask Stauffenberg:
When the twilight comes, will the sunlight be far away?

When the ropes of hangman
Could not hang the might of Resistance
I but chorus in glee
For the triumph of humanism

31. The Expectant

Two palms over the abdomen
Moaning to mitigate the pain
A life of limbo inheriting
The child in the belly protesting
The cot carries the wife of Amir
In the ominous kerosene flicker

The nameless begetter weary
His job shorn of the other day
Slams the door and spits the floor
Sits in a forsaken corner
Musing over the unwelcome bastard
Addition to the shoal of slaves!

The thoughts struck the fair
A distant groan at the frontier
A line of lightning passed the airs
The stars closed the shivering eyes
And count the passage of moments
A shriek of thunder winters the torments

Million pairs of hands varicose
Come forward and demand bellicose
Piercing the darkness of night
A twin arms of delivering might
A child in health born in filth
To break the fetters of age-old strength

The sight of the scene frightened
The humid heart of the dispossessed
Turns back in diffident dismay
To peep through the damned doorway
Nursing the hopes forlorn
The nature of the new born

32. The New Year Heralded in Dark

There is no new pen to write on the new dawn
As the pregnant experiences struggle to deliver
I wish to keep the new born to my bosom
But the bangs of past force me to behold the whimpers
And the lost drops of the bygones my paper venture to suck

I woke up in vigour and promise
I voyaged into the deep corners of human values
I tried to settle on the shores of faith and compassion
I thought my sweat and toil will bear fruit
I dreamt a smiling flower, a jasmine of crescents

My heart hangs in her locket
Which her begetter wants to replace
The legendary October, to me turned treacherous
As the birds of hope and flights of passion
Are shot down in the desert of humanity

There are no sails in the boats I anchored
No flowers in the gardens I nurtured
No smiles on the lips I feasted
There are only webs in the hairs I caressed
And the clouds of message defected to the gallery of gales

The twinkling stars lie under the sheet of darkness
The embryos of dunes sink to the table of waters
The rodents burrow deep into the springs of life
And the flowers of grass flew before seeding
A dagger thrust into me, lest I swim to the new shore

The seeds of my sunset
I fear I have sown myself
I burnt the oil of my heart in wait and vigil
But the morning star is too far to usher the chariot
And the new year heralded in dark

33. I Lead a Life of Perpetual Glory

Worn out by the termites of society
Ridden by the galloping mares of defeat
Trampled by the elephants of ill-luck
Eating the dead grain of the empty bowl
Drinking the waters of the barren rivers
Hearing the broken hearts of far east mothers
Seeing the fiendish dances of civilised inhumans
Indeed I lead a life of perpetual glory'

> The creatures of affluence promised me the glass of wine
> The dweller of the wayward street offered to quench my thirst
> The dog of the lane gave me a faithful friend
> The distant bird brought a song of spring
> The peacocks under the clouds lured me against the impending
> The cock of the morn broke its voice in time
> But the flames of the lords led me to the quicksand's
> Indeed I lead a life of perpetual glory.

The sun refused to shine at midnight
The stars twinkled in the mid-noon darkness
The books of wisdom asked me to be wise
They tell me to save my skin and soul
And be happy that I have their counsel
The knife on my back threatened to invite another
The soil under by hoe started to slide
Indeed I lead a life of perpetual glory.

But how can I have a fill of my belly
When the bellows of my fellow being tear my tympanum
But how can I accept the glass of water
When it belongs to the needy of my next door
The fires of society did not allow the thirsty
Even to drink their own tears
With burdensome stigma of a glorious heritage
Indeed I lead a life of perpetual glory.

34. The Contrast and the Conflict

The blind of the promising vision
Sways a starry vigil for the prophet of resurrection
Not a ray is wanting in her typhooned night
While in the broad spectrum of piercing light
A streak of darkness swallowed the mid-noon
And in the shrine of the summer day
The winter woods shone in black lustre
And the blinded woman paves her tumbling path.

The old maiden of the street
Silently offers the morning news
But the time lapsed without an inquisitive palm.
The age that should sit in respite
Struggles for her lurid stomach
Labours to convey the impending gloom
To the fellows grown thick with unconcern
A gloom that shall drown them to depths.

The lame on the road of sweat and blood
Ticking his cursed wooden steps
On the ground harder than the human heart
Leads the revolt of million legs
Against the rollers of incompassion
Having to loose nothing but the clutches
As the corpulent thighs peer through the windows
Breaking theirs on the silken beds.

The children necked out of the school
The trodden could not lick and pick for the fees
Their grandmother could not sell a sheet of news
To those who made and enjoy them
Their blind mother could not veer the eyes
From the ghastly darkness of the mid-noon
Their father could not lead a successful revolt
Against the fiendish ruffians of society

The brethren of the children born with shirts on
See the sight of the family's plight
The children caught in the web of contrasts
Bellow for help in the conflict of interests
As none push them to a leap of life
And flee away from the call of conscience.
But shall the contrasts ever remain
And the conflicts ever recoil?

35. Sans Life Farewell to Myself

Who are you?
Oh! who are you?
Damsel of the dreams, or
Child of nature's love

Tell me you are born for me
For, we met here without appointment
And meeting
You have not remained what you were
And I, what I was
Both lost on the same
Groping for each other
Like nectar in the flower
And sweetness in the nectar.

Tell me you will come with me
I shall build bridges
Over the brooks of desire
I shall fill the world
With the songs of heraldry
But the goals are on the cliff
Won't you sit in the saddle
And direct the gallop?

Who are you?
Oh! who are you?
Crest on the waves of sea, or
Movement of the peaceful sun kiss?

Promise me, you will drink my tears
I shall pour my agony over your head
Release my weight over your shoulders
Drink them and peep through the tight lips
The sea shall dry, and
Pearls beneath shall shine
Like the voice of the cuckoo
Like the song in that voice
You and me shall emerge.

Tell me you will breathe my laughter
I shall ripple your blood with joy
You shall be rocked in dance
And rolled in mirth
Ecstasy!
As the glow worms kindle our path
Your chariot shall shine in charms.

Who are you?
Oh! Who are you?
Star of the resplendent sky, or
The Light behind the dark cloud?

Promise me you will live with me
I shall build a home
My mother shall raise and wait
Foundations with her love
And walls with her blessings
Your mother shall raise the roof
And furnish the living
Life and lamp I shall give
and kindle you shall.
Passion shall bind us
Like the brightness of the moonlight
Peace shall dwell in us
Like the blue in the firmament.

Who are you?
Oh! Who are you?
Smile of Monalisa, Fresco of Ajanta
Sweetness of the child, or the calmness of sunkiss?

I am a red rose, I am a white rose
Red for endless love, white for spotless purity
I am a vagrant cloud
I am a falling cascade
Will you dare come with me
And breathe my life?
I shall fill the air with the music of our ticks
I shall lead the world in the shades of our steps.

36. I Wanted only to Live

I wanted only to live
In accord with the whispers of my blood
Promptings of my true self, and
Dictates of my conscience.
Why was that so very difficult?

The sands of shore
Eager to loll
When the waves bring the croons of love
But what of sands of dunes
The flying fragments
Visited ever not by the springs of life
But by gales of winds and clouds of white
Where written not a poem of promise
But inscribed in silver,
A warrant of typhoon.

I live in the void
My breaths are bubbles
Let me blow them off
My life is a cigarette
Let me burn on both ends.
Pack of chains and paste of puss
Dazed I stand
While the crocodiles of hate
And serpents of venom
Lounge in starry wait.

Summers sailed
Winters vanished
Autumns advanced.
Books of wisdom tell me:
Spring cannot be far away!
But my stones are hungry
My sands are thirsty
Bones of mind clamour
Bitter harvest, alluring sea
Trampling bulldozer, hot oven
Over my heavy heart
Cascades, cyclones and bees in my brain
Fate over my body, and
Fear over my limbs.
What use a flying cuckoo
Wingful and beautiful
Yet voiceless and fearful.

Wasted chances and humble yearnings
Waste lands and thirsty sands
Dumb pain depthless
Agony, ecstasy in ebb and tide
Fountains of invisible tears
My smiles harbour
I wailed for a handful of mercy
I cried for a fistful of tears
When I did not get
I commanded to shoot
But none behind to carry
I was ready to shoot
But none to command
Oh! world, Oh! Life
Why should you give me hope
And then kill it ?

I desired a stone
I wanted stillness
I desire to soil you with my tears
I long to breeze you with my laughter
Oh! Stagnant water
I wish to wave you with my rippling voice.
I longed for long hands and broad mind
To reach the newest horizons
I nurtured blazing eyes
And clarion tongue
In search of promise
To raise the call of dawn
But my hands were broken
And my wings were cut
Cataract squinted my vision
And my voice was drowned
In the strife of madness.

Half grown mankind!
A frog, a fish, a bird,
A serpent, a monkey,
In man together or separate
I prefer to live with
Than a half grown mankind
I hate. I detest.
When the wings of love
Fly at the mercy of feminine winds
When the springs of life
Are at the feet of whirlpools
What has years of life taught me?
In most of us
A resusciated brute waits for resurrection
In some of us
A redeemer nailed to the cross.

Lone and dark
On the thorny path of love
Yearning for the flower in the bush
Over the peak
Sightless, struggling to shed light
I burnt myself
Oh! fate tell me
What have you promised me
What have you given me?

My mother, my love
Hide me in your apron
Hug me to your neck
Today there is none for me.
Mother, I want you
To clay a stone
To breeze a stillness
Oh! Mother I want to sleep on your lap
In delirium, in peace
Eternal — my mother in your scabbard.

I wanted only to live
In accord with the whispers of my blood
Promptings of my true self, and
Dictates of my conscience
Why was that so very difficult?

37. Pulse of Life

I woke up with hope
And slept in despair, yet
I am the leader of my generation
I am the singer of my times
I am the prophet of my destiny

Only in the dreams of midnight
I realise the fruits of my aspirations
In the labour of the whole day
My eyes are drenched in sweat and blood, yet
I have faith in the promise of tomorrow

I voice the anguish around me
I know I fuel the fire in me
But why is my concern?
For the advent of dawn
For a peaceful tomorrow

Myriads of meaningful thoughts
Searching and toiling in my words
For an expression, for an identity

The sun is unborn in the life
But he is burning in my heart
So in the movements of 'niggers'
In Vietnam, and in Andes

The rays of progress cannot be extinguished
In any continent of the universe, for
My heir is the toiler longing for liberation

I am the sole hope left in this world
For the unfortunates of uncared wants
Devoured by pangs of hunger
The desires of the aborted virgin
The tears of mother throwing her still born
Swept off the air and slept in the soil

Trusting me for a future for their posterity
What if it is immature
What if it is ambiguous
I am throating the voice of the ages
While my heart is throbbing
With emotions and fervent hope.

I am the lightning power
Arising from the generator of this generation
Like the lamps of the past
I am not borne from the vacuum
Laying faith in the gods of the void

I can make the atom dance
Compel an electron to sing
And achieve a welfare state
I shall force the rocket
To inscribe the triumph of man
On the surface of moon.

What if I cease to breathe
Once I kindle a thousand candles
I am the spark of the ages
I am the power, I am the revolution
Emanating from the generator of this generation

38. Who Commands the Morning

Behind the highest walls
In the hardest sandy graveyard
From the witness of opacity
Of the ignoble metal unleashed
Are the elemental powers of fission
Through the wombs of men's brains.

From the pedestals of heavenly cabin
The goods of doom delivered safe
And triggered the ticks of last breath
With invitation descended the death
He who delivered is Homo sapiens
Recoiled are the remnants of ancestry.

Nobel, Lenin and Magsasay
Reduced to annual reminiscences
Prizes, Awards and Pughwashes
Are the sad remembrances
Of the blackest idea
Emanated from the whitest house.

Goaded on by fears, the fears of surrender
Drawn on by hopes, the hopes of conquest
Forced by challenge, the challenge of supremacy
Was created the Elixir, the elixir of elixirs!
But alas! Hanging everlasting
Damocles' legacy of New Mexico.

Gird up your loins
Oh men and women
Heartbeats of the Universe
Hopes of the posterity
Here is the answer
And you shall hearken to it.

Born in the primeval oceans, life and society
Endured the ebbs and tides in part and body
Changing and progressing since the remote millennia
Rose into harmonious unity through diversity
Man the Great, crowns the pinnacle
Is he for the society or the society for him?

Evils are the altruists in travesty
Individualism breeds them besides anarchy
Brothers and sisters, let us not
Bother the dead heaps of static arm - chairs
Who think and revel within the narrow limits
When the world is ever expanding.

With feet anchored in common man's earth
Hands raised into the inviting horizons
Mouths agape with rousing calls
The mountain does not wait for Mohammed
Shall we not hasten the proud waves of society
Shore the new beaches before the dusk sets in?

Gird up you loins
Oh men and women
Admixtures of contradictions
Instrumentals of less rationale
For I ask thee a question
And you shall answer me

> Who are the sinners? Scientists?
> The mere tools they turned out to be
> Their souls throbbing no death and doom
> Brain children orphaned and begetters discarded
> But how can we ignore Baldwin, when
> All the means of deluge are products of science.

Whose default ? For the urge of extinction
Of the atom or the Universe?
Of the death or the life?
Of the citizen or the state?
Of the individual or the society?
The fault lies with the existence of matter!
If not so, then is it of

> The Marxian economics or the Freudian sex?
> The proletarian discipline or the affluent anarchy?
> The cool practices or the holy precepts?
> The purpose or the lack of it?
> The fault lies in the futility of existence!

39. No Word said and no Tear Shed

I was a doctor and I lived for the poor
Disease fled when I appeared with my bag
The day prolonged its falls for my toils
The darkness trailed to keep me from the trivials
The Impossible tamed by my nurture
I saved the civilisation from the massacre of nature
While the gods of the heavens vied to garland
Nectar of blessings flowed from the far land.

> But no word said and no tear shed
> For the woman that nursed the ailing mattress
> The foundress that husbanded me in distress
> The angel that carved my bud to blossom
> Whose life I made a misery of boredom
> Whose rivers I dried for my glow
> Yet no word said and no tear shed.

I was a warrior and I lived to conquer
Foes ran from the ken of my shadow
The enemy dare not rub my name on the wall
Voices trembled to raise in front of me
People queued up to prostrate before me
Country after country followed suit

Inscribed in gold are the letters of my name
The citizens of my land cascaded to honour me
The warriors of the past stood up in their graves
The pens galloped the history with bucked up loins

But no word said and no tear shed
For the mother that fed me her bosomed courage
For the wife that served me the dish of her life
The friend that fused my back with pats of bravery
Yet no word said and no tear shed.

I was a scientist and I lived for knowledge
The intricacies of matter invited me to probe
In the test tube of my mind
I boiled the time over my burning heart
I toiled for the results that elevate the mankind
I rested in work and rusted in service
Centuries of bygones rose to see their happier posterity
The world applauded my achievement

But no word said and no tear shed
For the woman that spent a winkless life for my dawn
The mate that read, wrote and thought for me
My wife that assisted me in glorious discoveries
It is the one that I wrecked and deserted
Yet no word said and no tear shed.

I was a leader and I shook the world out of shackles
The agile exploiters forced to prostrate
The flag of freedom hoisted

I kindled optimism in the cursed
The peasants in the cremation ground
The labourers in the graveyard
The exploited and the tombed
Belaboured to behold the sight of their offsprings
Rendered a rare honour of justice

But no word said and no tear shed.
For my love that infused confidence in me
The beloved that awakened my sleeping soul!
The woman that made this man a giant
Who spent a restless life in this lifeless world
Yet no word said and no tear shed.

I was a scoundrel and I killed and looted
I left no integrity unpunished and no liberty ungagged
No law is sacred and honesty holy
The urchins feared to hear my name
No character could pass my street
I had feasts of women and I toppled the defiant
I established a reign of terror
The owls are my state birds
The sun ordered to beam out darkness
I won the people as my slaves
Eroding the foundations of sanity

They said that I could do so
For I have a woman behind!
None could realise I was a bachelor
Yet an untruth goes for a thing of shame

The people of the world worshipped me as a deity
The citizenry of the globe glorified me beyond measure
History conferred on me an enviable uniqueness
While the farmer dragged into the dusty dusk
While the weaver wailed in the worn out looms
While the labour was disinherited after the work
I ate ambrosia and treaded pearly paths
Clothes of finesse adorned my skin

And no word said and no tear shed
For the woman with the sickle in hand
And basket on the back
That brought the harvest to my mouth
Carrying the added weight of the world
For the woman with hammer in the fist
Breaking the stones lest they impede the path of man
Yet no word said and no tear shed.

40. God: A Great Necessity

Omnipresent! Omniscient! Omnipotent!

How nice it is to have a God.
No one sees god. But every one feels.
At least it is said

> It is like the bird that
> 'Feels the dawn when it is still dark'.
> It is also like the wolf
> That feels the dusk when there is still light.

The *Pancha Bhootas*, of nature were resources
When balanced, but very harmful if imbalanced.
Both good and bad are the attributes of the same.
Humans realised ecology and called it god.

> When a child is borne
> The mother feels the god.
> When some one dies,
> The dear ones fear the god.

When someone kills the other without touching him,
the witness sees the god.
God is not merely linkages, but a web, inscrutable.

> When bad people succeed and enjoy life,
> Why bad things happen to good people?
> What is god doing?
> Is he existing, or if not is he also bad like the powerful.
> God's duty is to protect the good and punish the evil.
> An enigma indeed.

God lies in the work.
Work produces dirt.
Cleanliness is next to Godliness.
Truth is god. But truth is bitter.
It takes us to the elegy land,
The last lap of all journeys, sooner.
God is a self contradiction

Myriad times I felt how nice if we have a god Albeit,
Formless, faceless, flavourless,
tasteless, speechless, senseless,
But valuable and powerful?
God is an insatiable yearning.

No one sees god, although feel, but late.
Therefore evils and bads, flourish.
How nice it is to have a God.

I have seen god,
In the first paragraph of
A Tale of Two Cities by Dickens.
And in the entire Siddhardha of Herman Hesse,
In Do Bigha Zameen taking Balraj townwards
And in Boot Polish when
David sings for rain, in Jail!

I feel god, whenever good happens,
Rain and river banks
I deny god, whenever bad happens, heat, dust, villainy
This is the stuff of god, a summation of all probabilities

But GOD has always haunted me
and did not enlighten me.
Ecology enlightens me.
And I found my God.
A great necessity.

If there is no God Invent One
- Voltaire

Poetry
A Product or Creation?

A. HOME WORKS

Triumph of Humanism

During the 1965-66 session I joined German classes. Learning a foreign language was a requirement for obtaining a Doctorate! Our Professor Lothar Wendel was a man of culture. His house was a Library-cum-Photo-museum I was often his guest. He embarked on writing a small book on German Civilisation. He wanted a tailpiece –a poem on his heroes – Herman Keyserling and Count Stauffenberg and offered his library for reference. After perusing for some time I picked up a few books, notably, Soldier's Revolt by Wolff. It tells the failed attempts on the life of Hitler by a group of highly decorated soldiers led by Count Stauffenberg who was then in the intimate trust of Hitler. It failed when some one inadvertently pushed the brief case with the bomb from his vicinity to a distance. Bomb exploded. But Hitler escaped with minor injuries. Conspirators were shot by a firing squad in a Quadrangle at the Military Head Quarters in Munchen.

The piece was written as a Homage to Count Stauffenberg who wanted to save the German Nation from its own leader!

Expectant

I used to walk every evening with Pranab Ray, my close friend and a classmate in Chromatography, Microbiology and Pharmacognacy classes and a few friends to a small local market- 'Connought' Place. During these times we would discuss current affairs of India and world. He was a student of M.Pharm, a distant nephew of Satyajit Ray but an admiring associate of Utpal Dutt in Calcutta. One day he was narrating the stories of Muslim infiltration from East Pakistan, flourishing Madrasas and the rise of religious fanaticism. We felt it was going to be a future menace, which became prophetic.

What is the remedy? Revolution – communistic - the one that brings all communities together. But what was going on in Bengal was merely rhetoric, theory, idealism without ability to transform. That was why the Naxalbari revolt that followed from this time, failed. Harekrishna Konar and Harikishen Singh Surjit, who returned from a secret trip from China, after meeting Mao also did not realise the basic ingredient of ushering a revolution – other than secrecy and doctrines. – The Physical Strength ! And roping in the otherwise unwilling Muslims into the movement was felt a necessity. Lack of Leftism by and large among Muslims everywhere became a historic scourge on the world, though communism in India was heralded chiefly by Muslims led by Muzaffar Ahmed, among others! So Karim, a Bangladeshi, and his yet to be born son became our topic-a futuristic piece appreciated by Ashim Chatterjee whom I met in Pranab's home a few years later. Incidentally the name Karim belongs to a dear classmate in my college.

Santal Woman

Those were the days of rumblings in the left-front in Bengal soon after their historic win in the elections. Marxist cadre were asking for sweeping reforms. Bhadralok were prevaricating. Suspicious of them revolt began in the minds of people, yearning for better deals, especially in the North and Eastern regions. The latter were well populated by the original people, the so-called tribals. The fiercely independent Santals. Jangal Santal became a rallying point. They were using women and children for confidential communications to avoid police repressions. Many such stories and sequels were narrated to me by my friend Pranab Ray, and asked me to write on them. The result was this piece

Pulse of Life

In 1965, Padmanabha Rao joined Commerce Department as a research scholar, resigning his lecturer post in Jedcharla, to do his doctorate under Dr. Dool Sing, who returned from MIT, USA after a two semester exposure.

He once told me of a great colleague to check our curiosity levels. Sure of this, he placed a Magazine, "Srujana", in front of us. Many glanced, perused and left. I persisted in going through. He told me of its Editor - his colleague at Jedcharla College. I subscribed for it and also for a few friends. In a later issue, he read a piece, Jeevanadi, authored by his friend, loudly. I was not impressed. He goaded - Why not you recite – a challenge clothed as a request – diplomatic as he was always. I did. He acknowledged I did better. The author, editor and his colleague was Varavara Rao.

One day, alone, I was reciting it loudly, pacing the room. Some friends – Pillai, Pranab Ray, Surendra Singh and Trivedi liked the rhythm, here and there. But how to explain the meaning, as they want. Another came in.

I explained line by line. They wanted a translation. I translated line by line; wherever English equivalents were wanting friends helped. The meaning of each stanza came out vividly, and in totality it was satisfactory. It read, progress is inevitable, it goes on, no matter the hurdles and breakdowns, the beats of hearts never end.

All dispersed. Soon after some sadness descended on me from far away Brahmin society. Helpless, returned to the room in Ram Bhavan. Wept for a while as was my frequent relief in those times. Took their scribbles, wetted a while, substituted some words. Everything fell in tune. Pranab came and saw - the only one so far. Varavara Rao to day is a Communist Revolutionary. A great soul. During Emergency I had to burn all the old issues of *Srujana*, a great little monthly. Sadly.

B. HOSPITAL WRITINGS

Spontaneous and Emotional

I was carried at midnight by my friends to the hospital suddenly afflicted by Gastroenteritis. When the body is weak, dehydrated thoughts go astray. Helplessness brings fond memories of lost people and sends us despondent and activates tear glands. At this juncture what passes on through your mind and heart tells you what you are! After an initial stay of a week, after several months, I had to be again hospitalised for another week. In all these 15 days, I must have read a few books and wrote considerably almost every day. They constitute about 10 pieces, retrieved in this collection.

Who Commands the Morning?

Dr. Choksi, sympathetic to my plight gave me a book, a great narration by Pearl. S. Buck, the American journalist and novelist, Nobel Laureate. It dealt with the Atomic Bomb Project carried out in New Mexico Desert under the leadership of Oppenheimer. The world's top scientists who took part in that were the characters in that. It was here that Oppenheimer exclaimed at the detonation and compared it to the Sun described in the Vedas! This was my inspiration for - Who Commands the Morning? My forebodings then, as an young man of 23 years with stars in the eyes and - of Nehru, came true ultimately – much to our chagrin and sorrow.

Others

One day, some one in the ward passed away, his young wife weeping inconsolably. Her hell began. A day latter the one on my side too died. Routinely the body was taken away, no one wept but for cutting sorry figures. There was enormous sadness descending on me. Dr. Choksi gave me another book, *The God that Failed* – It contained the tales of people like Koestler and Andre Gide who were led to communism by idealism and were frustrated by its practices and denounced it in later years. It was an eye opener to me – one who was gradually gravitating towards it in the very heart of the Citadel, a great capitalistic – Pilani, the native place of Birlas.

No matter what one does on this earth, one day it looses its value and even memory. No mater what you dream, realities could be different. But one has to keep on doing as per one's conscience. For this everyone needs a vocation, a hobby, an ideal dear to the heart, irrespective of livelihood chores. If both are same or match, life could be wonderful, for, one is seized by a passion all the time. Such feelings made me write a long prose that fell into poetic cadences, gradually.

By then I failed to enter the army as an Officer, in three attempts with SSB; then the goal shifted to become a Professor like my Godfather, B N Muley. This too appeared slipping with his death.

They shifted me to the children's ward. My neighbour was one Saboo, a student from the school, a scion of an industrialist family. Most of the time he will gossip about his friends and asks me what I was reading and writing. This rare curiosity, I never found again, that too coming from a boy born in riches and live and die in riches, only. Yet so much interest in people around. Doctors and Nurses thanked me for retaining him on his bed. Otherwise, he would be on rounds. Jayant Gupta told me that this boy requested the authorities not to inform his parents, lest they would carry him to Delhi, but wanted to be treated in this hospital.

C. SRI SRI'S MAHAPRASTHANAM

Inspirations and Translations many, only some remain, As I mentioned earlier the arrival of Padmanabha Rao as a research scholar brought considerable changes in me. One day he showed me a book, a slim one, *Maha Prasthanam, The Longest Journey*, written by Srirangam Srinivasa Rao, popularly known as Sri Sri, and asked me to read any page. Until then I had not heard of this collection of poems of different genres. He asked me to read loudly, Then I found that they had a rhythm with in. I did not understand the meanings of many words. I read more pages, then loudly. I enjoyed it immensely. Thus, I got hooked to that book, and forever.

Sri Sri became my Guru. And Padmanabha Rao who introduced me, became a Guruji.

It became an encore, a routine for me to read the poetic pieces loudly every day in my room when no one was around in the hostel corridor in Ram Bhavan. One day Surendra Singh came to see me and heard it from outside. Pleasantly mischievous, he brought some friends to listen to me from the vicinity. Thus, began another chapter in my daily chores. Some friends would come only to enjoy the style and rhythm of my recitation and imitate me, to poke fun. But some asked me to tell the meaning, and others to translate. Gopala Krishna Pillai and Sweta Kurup told that the pieces resembled Vallathol, the great poet in Malayalam; Basant Tiwari felt they resemble compositions of Ram Dhari Singh Dinkar; Shahabuddin said Sahir Ludhianvi wrote similarly. Pranab said similar writings came in Bengali from Sukanto Bhattacharya. His poetry was also recited loudly, set to music and then to dance, subsequently. My friend Kanchan Mojumdar told me that they came as cassettes and CDs. I had the good fortune of seeing a young man performing a fantastic dance to a revolutionary song of Sukanto. Alas! Sukanto died at 25!

Coming back to the main stream of narration. This pastime lead me to translate some of Sri Sri's Poetic pieces. Among many recited and translated, whenever demanded by friends, I could retrieve from my archives only some! They are here:

D. PRANAB RAY

In a few cases it has so happened that Pranab told me a story, a theme, and I wrote as heart-felt as possible; improved it and then split into poetic notes. Then the vocabulary and figures of speech. Santal woman, Expectant etc, come in this category. The large varieties too – assays modified into poetic design. Pranab was a great asset and creative to core.

E. CUT AND PASTE

One can write tellingly. Another can write movingly on some subjects, as pet themes and certain times. Then scissor the prose into pieces, of smaller dimensions. Yes, a poem is made!

ART OF SHEKHAWAT, AND A HEARTLESS VISITOR

All my poetry was written in Pilani. In those years I was also asked to teach. One student who is an artist like his father before was so much fascinated that he volunteered to make sketches appropriate to each poem. We together laboured to make poems hand written and he would make sketches with pencil. A marvelous book emerged by the efforts of Shekhawat. The book traveled with me everywhere and admired by everyone who saw it. But in Puducherry it disappeared. Some heartless student or a visiting teacher just pilfered it with a smile. Most sins are committed due to the gullibility of the victim.

Author's Works

1. SHARKS ON CAMPUS, Tragicomedy of Indian Universities, p. 371, 2015 - Notion Press
2. ECOLOGY, ENVIRONMENT AND POLITICS, p. 412, 2018 – Gyan Publications
3. TEACHING LABOURS OF SISIPHUS. VOL. 1. p. 425, 2019 - Gyan Publications
4. TEACHING LABOURS OF SISIPHUS. VOL. 2. p. 381, 2020 - Gyan Publications
5. IRRIGATION TANKS OF SEMI- ARID ECOSYSTEMS. p. 393, 2020 - Gyan Publications
6. GLOBALIZATION and ECOPHAGY – 1, Chemicals, Mutations and Gene-Epidemics, Gen-Next Publications, p. 204, 2020.
7. SO THE TIME PASSED AWAY. P 92, 2021, - Gyan Publications

In Press

8. *AUTOECOGRAPHY OF STOLEN FUTURES - 1*
9. GLOBALIZATION and ECOPHAGY – 2,
   Episode at Vizag –Repetition of Bhopal Tragedy

If Health and Energy Permit, the following Files may become books if assistancs becomes available

10. *AUTOECOGRAPHY OF STOLEN FUTURES-2*
11. *AUTOECOGRAPHY OF STOLEN FUTURES-3*
12. ECOGRAPHY OF TAMIL NADU COAST FOR DEVELOPMENT
13. PIRANHAS AMONG INTELLECTUALS AND INDIAN NATIONHOOD

50 years passed since my studenthood. Current society and the practice of politics reminds me the warning of Churchill on indian intelligentia 74 years ago in the house of Commons

POWER WILL GO TO THE HANDS OF RASCALS, ROGUES, FREEBOOTERS

ALL INDIAN LEADERS WILL BE OF LOW CALIBER & MEN OF STRAW

THEY WILL HAVE SWEET TONGUES AND SILLY HEARTS

THEY WILL FIGHT AMONGST THEMSELVES FOR POWER

INDIA WILL BE LOST IN POLITICAL SQUABBLES

A DAY WOULD COME WHEN EVEN AIR & WATER WOULD BE TAXED IN INDIA

Dr. Samuel Johnson's Appeal to the fellow writers

Dr. Samuel Johnson, wrote an open letter to all writers of Great Britain appealing them to conclude their creations positively, optimistically and hopefully to please the readers and their listeners. Because evil and wicked alone triumph, not the good and virtue. Let the people atleast live in hope, which also contributes to happiness.